PRAYER
OUR SECRET WEAPON

PAIILINE HARDING

Copyright © 2013 Pahline Harding

Scriptures are taken from the NIV (New International Version) © 1973 of the bible. Used by Permission

All rights reserved.
No part of this publication may be reproduced or transmitted in any form or by any means, electronic or mechanical, including photocopy, recording on any information storage or retrieval system, without permission in writing from the publisher.

CONTENTS

Introduction: Our Secret Weapon	5
1. Praise and Thanksgiving	8
2. Prepare Yourself for Action	12
3. Pray for Those Over You	17
4. Petitions	20
5. Promoting the Family	24
6. Pray for Healing	29
7. Protection and Wisdom	34
8. Passion for Souls	38
9. Pray for Your City	42
10. Planet Shaker	45
11. Power of Heaven	49
12. Personal Portion from God	52

OUR SECRET WEAPON

He trains my hands for battle,
my arms can bend a bow of bronze.
You armed me with strength for battle.

As for me, I cry to God,
And the Lord saves me.
He rescues me unharmed
from the battle waged against me,
Even though many oppose me!
2 Samuel 22:35 & 40 Psalm 55:16-18

Prayer is the most powerful weapon we have at our disposal. God has provided the gift of prayer as a means to move Heaven and earth.

God did not leave us as Christians in this world without the means to overcome in life. Jesus Himself was our example of how prayer brought God's Kingdom to earth.

Jesus spent much time in prayer and communication with God. There are many ways we can pray and this book is an aid to get started and by no means exhaustive.

The subjects for prayer here are scriptural and useful for our everyday lives.

You can pray through the prayer points for as long or as short as you like. The important thing to do before you begin to pray is to ask the Holy Spirit to lead you and hear what God is saying on each section.

Do not allow your weapons to go rusty but pray constantly and see God do amazing things through you!

An army marches on its prayers!

Before You Pray!

It is important to remember these three things when you pray:

There must be a target or focus for your prayers.
No archer simply shoots an arrow in the air; they aim for a target and a goal. Prayer is a powerful weapon that needs to be used skilfully and wisely to obtain the best results.

Ask yourself what the focus of your prayer is and what are you really asking God for? Aim very precisely. Like an archer they stand focused for a long time before shooting to get an accurate result. Be specific in prayer and don't generalise. The more simple and specific your prayers the better for God does not need long words and sentences; He is listening to your heart.

Faith must be present when praying. Jesus said believe that you have what you pray for and receive it by faith. Faith that God is hearing and answering your prayer is essential.

You need to ask as though you have already received your prayer.

Use scripture and the promises of God as often as possible in your prayers. Do not pray the problems to God but pray the solutions from the Word of God. Do not forget to remind God of His wonderful promises.

Pray in the Spirit on all occasions with all kinds of prayers and requests. Be alert and always keep on praying for all the Lord's people. Ephesians 6:18

CHAPTER ONE

PRAISE AND THANKSGRIVING

Enter His gates with thanksgiving and His courts with Praise. Psalm 100:4

It is good to begin our time with God in thanksgiving for what He has done and praise Him for Who He is.

Thank Him for as many things as possible and in different ways. Psalm 149: 1-5 exhorts us to praise Him with the dance, music and song. Do not let your thanks and praise get boring for you or God.

Thanksgiving

Give thanks in all circumstances, for this is God's will for you in Christ Jesus. Give thanks to the Lord, for He is good.

Let us come before Him with thanksgiving and extol Him with music and song.

But thanks be to God! He gives us the victory through our Lord Jesus Christ. Let us be thankful and so worship God with reverence and awe.

1 Thess 5:18 Psalm 136:1 Psalm 95:2
1 Corinthians 15:57 Hebrews 13:28

Some areas For Thanksgiving!

Thank Him for:

God's salvation through Christ
His provision
His protection
Eternal life
Victory
His deliverance
His angels with you
His good plans for you
Christ's death on the cross
His Love for you
His blood - forgiveness - healing
Life
Strength

Family: Spouse – children – parents etc.
Food
Weather
Home
Neighbours
People's kindness
Open doors
Friends
Work Opportunities
The government
Your pastor
Your church
Your city – town – country
Education
Hospitals – Police – Universities – Courts
Transport

(The list is endless but this will get you started)

9

Praise Him For Who He Is!

The Alpha and Omega
The Beginning and the End
The Desire of all Nations
The Bright and Morning Star
Our Intercessor
High Priest
Lion of Judah
Lamb of God
Captain of the Hosts
King of Kings
Lord of Lords
Our Righteousness
Our Healer
Our Saviour
Redeemer
The Resurrection
The Way the Truth and the Life
Prophet
Pearl of Great Price
Wonderful – Altogether Lovely
The Shepherd of our Souls
The True Vine
The Water of Life
The Bread of Life
The Great I Am
Faithful and True
Our Exceeding Great Reward
Anointed One
Captain of the Lord's Hosts
Bridegroom
The Door
Our Deliverer
Our Advocate
Our Peace
Our Wisdom
The Author and Finisher of our Faith
Delight
Image of the Invisible God - Most Holy
Mighty to Save
Judge
Jesus the Lamb of God, who takes away the sin of the world.

Praise

Praise the Lord
Praise God in His sanctuary
Praise Him in His mighty heavens
Praise Him for His acts of power
Praise Him for His surpassing greatness
Praise Him with the sounding of the trumpet
Praise Him with the harp and lyre
Praise Him with timbrel and dancing
Praise Him with the strings and pipe
Praise Him with the clash of cymbals
Praise Him with resounding cymbals.

Let everything that has breath praise the Lord.
Praise the Lord!

Psalm 150

CHAPTER TWO

PREPARE YOURSELF FOR ACTION!

Let us take a moment to examine ourselves in the light of scripture and present ourselves to God afresh today.

Let us then approach God's Throne of Grace with confidence, so that we may receive mercy and find grace to help us in our time of need.

Therefore, brothers and sisters, since we have confidence to enter the Most Holy Place by the blood of Jesus, by a new and living way opened for us through the curtain, that is, His body, and since we have a great priest over the house of God, let us draw near to God with a sincere heart and with the full assurance that faith brings, having our hearts sprinkled to cleanse us from a guilty conscience and having our bodies washed with pure water.

Search me, God, and know my heart, test me and know my anxious thoughts. See if there is any offensive way in me.

If we confess our sins, He is faithful and just and will forgive us our sins and purify us from all unrighteousness.

And when you stand praying, if you hold anything against anyone, forgive them, so that your father in Heaven may forgive you your sins.

Brothers and sisters, do not slander one another.

God opposes the proud but shows favour to the humble. Submit yourselves then to God. Resist the devil and he will flee from you. Come near to God and He will come near to you. Humble yourselves before the Lord, and He will lift you up.

Have mercy on me, oh God, according to your unfailing love, according to your great compassion blot out my transgressions. Wash away all my iniquity and cleanse me from my sin.

But you were washed, you were sanctified, you were justified in the name of the Lord Jesus Christ and by the Spirit of our God.

Those who have had a bath need only to wash their feet; their whole body is clean. And you are clean!

Hebrews 4:16	Psalm 139:23-24
Hebrews 10:19	Mark 11:22-25
1 John 1:9	Psalm 51:1-2
1 John 1:9-10	1 Corinthians 6:11
James 4:6-10	John 13:10

Come Clean

Jesus said those who had a bath needed only to wash their feet. This meant that when we become Christians we are made holy and righteous through what Christ has done for us on the cross and God looks on us as holy. However, in our everyday life our souls are in a process of being changed and we can grieve the Holy Spirit who lives in us when we sin.

Therefore, to keep powerful in the Holy Spirit we need to keep shorts accounts with God and be quick to say sorry for any wrongdoing.

It is good to take a few moments and bring anything to God that is causing you to lose your peace and joy. The kingdom of God is righteousness, peace and joy in the Holy Spirit.

Is there someone who has hurt or offended you in any way? Take a moment to give the pain and the offence to God and allow Him into the situation. He knows you are hurting and wants to heal the wound. Be willing to forgive and let God deal with the situation.

Give Him your struggles and areas of weakness and receive His strength to overcome. The battle is not yours it is the Lord's and He will fight for you.

Be willing to give up your pride and submit to whatever God is asking of you at this time.

When you fall at His feet; He lifts you up to new heights.

Do not fall into condemnation. Repentance means being honest with God being forgiven and moving on in the power of the Holy Spirit.

If you have offended anyone or spoken bad about someone take the opportunity to make amends and know God's healing.

Remember: where sin increased, grace increased all the more! Romans 5:20

A Prayer of Preparation

Dear Father,
You know me and love me. Please cleanse me today from any sin I have committed by the blood of your son Jesus. If I have wronged You or anyone else knowingly or unknowingly I repent and ask for forgiveness.
I forgive those who have hurt or offended me especially ....for..
I ask for the power and cleansing of the Holy Spirit in my life to live for you today.
Thank you that Jesus is my Holiness.
In Jesus Name

Be open to anything the Holy Spirit may want to say to you at this point.

God stays close to the humble.

CHAPTER THREE

PRAY FOR THOSE OVER YOU

Submit yourselves for the Lord's sake to every human authority.

I urge, then first of all, that petitions and thanksgiving be made for all people for kings and all those in authority.

Remember your leaders, who spoke the word of God to you.

Honour your mother and father which is the first commandment with a promise so that it may go well with you and that you may enjoy long life on the earth.

Wives submit to yourselves to your own husbands as you do to the Lord.

1 Peter 2:13
1 Timothy 2:1

Hebrews 13:7
Ephesians 6:1

We are called by God to respect and pray for those in authority over us.

The Monarchy
The Government
Employers
Our Pastors and Ministers
Leaders and Teachers
Our Spouse
Our Parents

The measure in which we honour those God has placed over us will be the measure God is able to honour us.

We only walk in authority if we are submitted to those in authority over us.

God appoints leaders, therefore, we need to respect their position and pray for them.

A Prayer For Leaders

Dear Father,
I speak blessing and honour over those you have placed over me and trust you with their leadership.
May you grant them protection, peace and wisdom in exercising their authority and keep them from the snare of the enemy.
I pray for those in authority over me especially
....
And I pray you would give them vision, integrity and wisdom in their God given positions and always keep them accountable to You. Please make me a blessing to them, In Jesus Name.
Amen

Who being in very nature God, did not consider equality with God something to be used to His own advantage; rather He made Himself nothing by taking the very nature of a servant.   Philippians 2:1-11

CHAPTER 4

PETITIONS

Do not be anxious about anything, but in every situation, by prayer and petition, with thanksgiving, present your requests to God.

Cast all your anxiety on Him because He cares for you.

Cast your cares on the Lord and He will sustain you.

Do not worry about your life, what you will eat or drink; or about your body, what you will wear. Do not worry about tomorrow. But seek first His kingdom and His righteousness, and all these things will be given to you as well.

Ask and it will be given to you; seek and you will find; knock and the door will be opened to you.

You may ask me for anything in my name, and I will do it.

This is the confidence we have in approaching God; that if we ask anything according to His will, He hears us. And if He hears us, whatever we ask, we know that we have what we asked of Him.

We know that in all things God works for the good of those who love Him, who have been called according to His purpose.

God who richly provides us with everything we need for our enjoyment.

Philippians 4:6   John 14:14
1Peter 5:6   1 John 5:14
Psalm 55:22   Romans 8:28
Matthew 6:25   Mark 4:38-41   1
Matthew 7:7   Timothy 6:17

No Worries

Worries and anxieties can consume us and we can spend our mental, physical and spiritual energy worrying about things that may not happen.

God does not want us going through life anxious, worried or burdened with lots of cares. God wants us free to enjoy Him and has provided a place to cast off the weight of our cares. He says to cast or throw all our cares, worries and burdens on to Him.

If we have the ability to change the things we are worrying about we should make a plan for change. However, if our worries are about things out of our control then we should give them to God and trust that He will act for us.

God does not want us walking about unhappy and worried all the time. Sometimes we are not aware of how much we are worrying until we begin to bring them all to God. Most people find they have many challenging situations going on at one time.

Writing down a list of the things that are weighing heavy on me has always helped me, I am then able to pray through the list and feel much lighter at the end of the prayer.

These are some of the concerns we all face which could go down on our list:

Health   Relationships
Family   Money
Work   Future
Church.

Take a moment to write a list or simply go to prayer and list One by One the things worrying you and pray:

Dear Father,
Thank you for your faithfulness and the promise that You will never, never fail me or forsake me. Thank you that you promise to work all things together for my good. I come to You and give you the cares and worries of my heart which are..
Thank you that according to your word you are concerned about every situation that concerns me. As I have released all my worries to you, I now repent of my worry and command all anxieties weighing on me to go right now in Jesus Name. Amen.

You will keep in perfect peace those whose minds are steadfast on You.

And the peace of God, which transcends all understanding, will guard your hearts and your minds in Christ Jesus.

Isaiah 26:3   Philippians 4:7

CHAPTER FIVE

PROMOTING THE FAMILY

Prayer for the family.

So in Christ Jesus you are all children of God through faith for you are all one in Christ Jesus.

I will send the prophet Elijah to you before that great and dreadful day of the Lord comes. He will turn the hearts of the parents to the children and the hearts of the children to their parents.

Has not the one God made you? And what does the Lord require? Godly offspring. So be on your guard and do not be unfaithful to the wife of your youth.

He who finds a wife finds what is good and receives favour from the Lord.

A wife of noble character who can find? She is worth more than rubies. She is clothed with strength and honour, she can laugh at the days to come. Honour her for all that her hands have done.

All your children will be taught by the Lord and great will be their peace.

Sing barren woman, you who never bore a child, because more are the children of the desolate woman.

For I have chosen him, so that he will direct his children and his household after him to keep the way of the Lord by doing what is right and just, so that the Lord will bring about for Abraham what He has promised him.

Children are a heritage from the Lord, offspring a reward from Him. Your wife will be like a fruitful vine within your house. Your children will be like olive shoots around your table.

Children obey your parents in the Lord, for this is right.

Honour your father and mother so that it may go well with you.

Submit to one another out of reverence for Christ. Husbands love your wives as Christ loved the church. Wives submit yourselves to your own husbands as you do to the Lord.

Fathers do not exasperate (incite to anger, irritate, provoke to rage) your children, but bring them up in the instruction of the Lord.

Galatians 3:26	Isaiah 54:1
Malachi 4:5	Genesis 18:19
Malachi 2:15	Psalm 127:3
Proverbs 18:22	Psalm 128:3-6
Proverbs 31:10	Ephesians 6:1-4

FAMILY

A godly family is the focus of God's heart and plans. God wants families to perpetuate His love, faith and godliness. God has been in the business of families ever since Adam and Eve and the beginning of time. God ordained that His legacy would live on through the family.

God loves you and your family and He has planned the very best for you. He knows the battles you face as a family and will stand with you and fight for you. Prayer is our weapon against the forces of darkness that would seek to destroy us.

Decree and speak out every day the family you want to see in God. You can walk in authority against the power of the enemy for your family and nothing shall by any means harm you.

Commit your family to prayer and seek God's protection and grace over them. If they are not saved pray for their salvation and speak God's good plans over their lives.

Refuse to accept any plan but God's for your family and bring them before the throne of God and present them to God.

Pray for refreshing waters for your marriage and commit your spouse to God and bless them. Do not allow complaining about them to enter your prayer life.

Thank God for your family and ask Him to redeem any areas you feel have been lost to the enemy.

Never, ever give up praying for your family. You will reap great rewards.

A Decree for your Family

I decree over my marriage that a three-fold cord is not easily broken.
My children are a heritage and a blessing from the Lord.
My children are taught of the Lord and great is their peace.
I decree my family shall fulfil their God given destinies and follow the Lord.
They shall be for signs and wonders and a testimony to the grace and glory of God.
Any power of the enemy shall be broken over their lives and no weapon fashioned against them shall prosper.
Our family is blessed and a blessing to many.
Our redeemer lives!

A Prayer for the Family

Dear Father,
I bring my family before you today and ask for your divine protection and covering over our relationships, destinies and walk with you.
I pray the covering of the blood over us and ask that your angels surround us in our daily lives.
I ask that you would bring healing to the relationships in our family and that your grace would abound where there has been sin. I pray we would grow in your love and understanding for one another.
Please give us wisdom in these days in every aspect of family life that we may do what is right before you.
I pray for the salvation of those who do not know you in my family especially ....
and pray they would come to know you as their saviour.

Please guide us as a family that we may know the way forward and keep in step with you. Fill us as a family with the Holy Spirit that we may walk in your power and strength. May we be a blessing to many and bring glory to You.

In Jesus Name, Amen

CHAPTER SIX

PRAY FOR HEALING

Surely, He took our pain and bore our suffering and by His wounds we are healed.

Heal me, Lord, and I will be healed.

A large crowd followed Him and He healed all who were ill.

Forget not all His benefits: who forgives all your sins and heals all your diseases.

Jesus went throughout Galilee healing every disease and sickness among the people.

For I am the Lord who heals you.

Is any among you sick? Let them call the elders of the church to pray over them and anoint them with oil. The prayer offered in faith will make the sick person well.

He gave them authority to drive out impure spirits and to heal every disease and sickness.

He healed those who needed healing.

He heals the broken hearted and binds up their wounds.

I will heal their backsliding

The word of the Lord was present to heal.

This is what the Lord, the God of your father David, says: 'I have heard your prayer and seen your tears; I will heal you. I will add fifteen years to your life.'

My flesh and my heart may fail, but God is the strength of my heart and my portion forever.

Isaiah 53: 4-5	Exodus 15:26	Hosea 14:4
Jeremiah 17:5	James 5:14	Luke 5:17
Matthew 12:15	Matthew 10:1	2 Kings 20:5
	Luke 9:11	Psalm 73:26
Psalm 103:3	Peter 2:24	
Matthew 4:23	Psalm 147:3	

Does God heal?   Yes!
Does God heal today? Yes!

God has chosen to heal us through the power of His Son Jesus. When Jesus died on the cross He did not only forgive us for our sins but He healed our bodies from the effects of sin and the world.

God does not only want to heal us spiritually but physically and emotionally as well. Jesus said He was anointed to heal the broken hearted and bind up their wounds.

Often our bodies suffer as a result of our emotions getting damaged so God wants to heal every part of us.

The word says, By His stripes we are healed'. Jesus healed many people in the Bible and many people today testify of being healed in Jesus.

Stand on the promises of God's word if you need healing and ask God to send His word to heal you today. Do not give up because you have asked God to heal you and you are still sick: delay is not denial. Keep knocking and asking, maybe God wants to show you something important linked to your healing or life. Be open to hear what God is saying to you.

Maybe you have known God's healing and the symptoms have returned. Stand you ground and command all symptoms to go in Jesus' Name. You are not alone in your battle with sickness; Jesus is with you and will never fail you or forsake you.

Trust Him for your healing. Speak the word of God over yourself.
Always remember to forgive anyone you need to.
Ask the elders of your church to anoint you with oil according to James 5.
Praise Jesus that He is your healer.
Pray for others who are sick and build your faith.

Your confession of faith has powerful results.

A Decree for Healing

I decree that by the stripes of Jesus I am healed, spiritually, physically and emotionally. Nothing shall by any means harm me.
I am a covenant child of God through the blood of Jesus and I stand on the promises of God's word for my healing.
My heart is strong, my bones are strong and my mind is strong.
I will not die but live and declare the works of God.
According to your word I am forgiven and healed of all my diseases and redeemed from destruction. My youth is renewed as the eagles.
Lord you have blessed my food and water and have taken sickness away from me. Therefore, I will fulfil the number of my days in health.
I resist the enemy in every form that He comes against me and I command my body to be strong and healthy in Jesus Name.

A Prayer for healing

Dear Father,
Thank you for providing healing through your son Jesus.
Thank you that by His stripes we are healed.

I thank you Father that my body is the temple of the Holy Spirit and your healing life flows through me. Father, I confess my faults to you today and forgive all those who have hurt me in any way. Please heal me today from ....
in the name of your son the Lord Jesus Christ. I take authority over the root of sickness and disease in my body and command it to go in Jesus Name. Thank you for my healing and strength, please fill me afresh with the Holy Spirit.

I pray for others who need your healing especially
....
Please heal them from ....and fill them with your life giving spirit. Deliver them from all evil and restore them to full health and strength.
In Jesus Name,
Amen.

Your daily medicine: Eat healthy, think healthy and speak healthy!

CHAPTER SEVEN

PROTECTION AND WISDOM

Get wisdom at any cost!

If any of you lacks wisdom you should ask God who gives generously to all.

The Benefits of Wisdom:

Those who are wise will shine like the brightness of the heavens.

You will understand the fear of the Lord.

You will be promoted.

You will have more profit than gold, silver or rubies.

You will have nothing that compares with her.

You will have long life.

You will have riches and honour.

Your ways will be pleasant.

Your paths will be peaceful.

You will be kept from adultery.

You will have a tree of life.

You will be blessed.

Your head will wear a garland and a crown.

You will walk in safety.

Your foot will not stumble.

Your sleep will be sweet and you will be unafraid.

You will be protected and saved from wicked men.

You will be honoured.

Daniel 12:3   James 1:5   Proverbs 2-3

Cry out for Wisdom!

The Word of God emphasises how important it is to seek and obtain wisdom from God. You need more than intellectual wisdom; you need wisdom and understanding that comes from above.

You are not encouraged to 'ask' for wisdom but to 'cry out' and be desperate about needing the wisdom of God in your life. The more you ask for wisdom the more you will receive it.

God says He will give wisdom generously and will not rebuke us for it. God wants you to have the ability to make wise decisions in every situation you face. His wisdom will help you work through suffering and trials and discern right from wrong.

The only requirement needed to receive God's wisdom is to believe He will give it to you. Wisdom is not given on your merit but it is given to those who ask for it

Wisdom that comes from heaven is first of all pure; then peace-loving, considerate, submissive, full of mercy and good fruit, impartial and sincere. James 3:17

A Prayer for Wisdom:

Dear Father,
I thank you that Jesus is my wisdom and that the wisdom of God flows through me. I ask you Father God for a generous supply of wisdom for every situation I am going to face today.

I ask for your wisdom for work, church, relationships, finance, family and health. I especially ask for wisdom for ....
I pray that I may walk in wisdom in all I say and do, especially in making decisions.

May your wisdom manifest in every area of my life and may the blessings of wisdom be released over me.
May I be a source of wisdom to all I come in contact with and the words of my mouth speak with supernatural wisdom.

Give me a heart that would cry out for your wisdom, instead of relying on my own understanding.
Thank you that your wisdom is my protection and promotion.
In Jesus Name,

Amen.

CHAPTER EIGHT

PASSION FOR SOULS

The one who saves souls is wise.

Those who lead many to righteousness will shine like the stars forever and ever.

Jesus said, 'Go and make disciples of all nations, baptising them in the name of the Father and of the Son and of the Holy Spirit.'

For I am not ashamed of the gospel, because it is the power of God that brings salvation to everyone who believes.

He sent them out to proclaim the kingdom of God and to heal the sick.

Preach the word; be prepared in season and out of season.

The Lord is not slow in keeping His promise; instead He is patient with you, not wanting anyone to perish, but everyone to come to repentance.

The Spirit of the Lord is on me, because he has anointed me to preach good news to the poor.

How can they hear without someone preaching to them?

Woe to me if I do not preach the gospel.

Through Him we received grace and apostleship to call all the Gentiles to the obedience that comes from faith for His name's sake.

And even if our gospel is veiled, it is veiled to those who are perishing. The god of this age has blinded the minds of unbelievers, so that they cannot see the light of the gospel that displays the glory of Christ, who is the image of God. For what we preach is not ourselves, but Jesus Christ as Lord.

Proverbs 11:30	2 Peter 3:9
Daniel 12:3	Luke 4:18
Matthew 28:16	Romans 10
Romans 1:16	1 Corinthians 9:16
Matthew 2	Romans 1:5
2 Timothy 4:2	2 Corinthians 4:3-5

God is passionate about souls and He wants us to share His passion.

God loved the world so much that He gave His only begotten son. That whoever believes in Him should not perish but have eternal life. It is not God's will that any on the earth should perish without the knowledge of Him.

He wants every Christian to win others for Him. He wants us to be active partners with the Holy Spirit to win the world for Jesus. There are many ways to share your faith and the gospel.

Pray for those who do not know Jesus. Pray on your own or with others.

Share your testimony of how you became a Christian with family and friends. Write out your testimony in about 200 – 300 words and have it printed up and available to give to those who ask you.

Invite people to Church to hear the gospel.

Invite people to your home or for coffee to share the Gospel.

Get involved in an evangelistic programme at church or go on a mission.

Love people into the knowledge of Christ.

A prayer for souls

Dear Father,
Thank you that Jesus died for the whole world. I ask that you would make me a soul winner and give me divine opportunities to share your gospel.
I pray for the salvation of those who do not know you, especially ....
I pray their eyes may be opened to see Jesus and their ears to the truth of your word.

May your Holy Spirit convict them of sin and convince them of the truth of the Gospel of Jesus Christ.

I call them out of darkness into your light and pray they will be released from the north, south, east and west. I bind the enemy from blinding their eyes and any hold He has over them.

I ask protection for them and their families. May they be released to be able to make a decision for You,
In Jesus Name,

Amen.

CHAPTER NINE

PRAY FOR YOUR CITY

Seek the peace and prosperity of the city to which I have carried you. Pray to the Lord for it, because if it prospers, you too will prosper.

Then Abraham said, 'May the Lord not be angry, but let me speak just once more. What if only ten can be found there?' He answered, 'For the sake of ten, I will not destroy it.'

Jeremiah 29:7   Genesis 18:32   2 Samuel 20:21

One can make a Difference!

One man pleaded for a city and God heard him.
One woman acted wisely and she saved a whole city.

You can make a difference where you live.
Ask God to give you favour with the local authorities etc
Pray for your city and the place where you live. Pray for its leaders and the institutions there. Ask God for opportunities to serve and make a difference where you live.

Bless your area, the people who live there and the leaders. Bless the shops, the schools, places of work. Pray for the prosperity of your city and be a blessing to your area. Any area should be blessed when God's people are praying for it.

A prayer for your city

Dear Father,
I thank you for where I live and especially for the blessings of ....
(thank God for the good things where you live)

I ask that you would bless my town and city and I pray for peace and prosperity to be found here. I pray that your people would be a light in this place and righteousness would prevail.

I pray for the sake of your people here you would bless and not bring judgment.

I pray for a move of God in this city and that many would turn to you.

Please make me a carrier of your presence and blessing as I live and work here in this place.

I ask for the heart of Abraham that would cry out for my city and people.

Please help me make a difference in this place,
In Jesus Name,

Amen.

CHAPTER TEN

PLANETSHAKERS!

To the Ends of the Earth

Ask Me, and I will make the nations your inheritance, the ends of the earth your possession.

But you will receive power when the Holy Spirit comes on you and you will be my witnesses in Jerusalem, and in Judea and Samaria, and to the ends of the earth.

All the peoples on earth will be blessed through you.

You will rule over many nations but none will rule over you.

My house will be called a house of prayer for all nations.

Nations will come to your light.

Look around from where you are, to the north and south, to the east and west. All the land that you see I will give to you and your offspring forever.

The Lord has driven out before you great and powerful nations; to this day no one has been able to withstand you. One of you routs a thousand because the Lord your God fights for you just as He promised.

All the ends of the earth will remember and turn to the Lord, and all the families of the other nations will bow down before Him. For dominion belongs to the Lord and He rules over the nations.

I appointed you as a prophet to the nations.

Your name will be Abraham for I have made of you a father of many nations. Her name will be Sarah. I will bless her so that she will be the mother of nations, Kings of peoples will come from her.

For the earth will be filled with the knowledge of the Lord as the waters cover the sea.

Psalm 2:8	Isaiah 60:3	Jeremiah 1:5
Acts 1:7	Genesis 13:14	Genesis 16:5
Genesis 12:3	Joshua 23:9	Isaiah 11:9
Deut 15:6	Psalm 2:27	Ezekiel 39:21
Mark 11:17		

Ask for the nations!

The Holy Spirit was given to us to take and possess the whole earth. We can ask for the nations in prayer and see God move in those areas.

Are you interested in a country or countries? Then start by praying for it. God wants your blessing and influence to go further than your own doorstep.

If you cannot go personally to the different nations you can certainly influence them by your prayers. God will show you how your prayers can make a difference.

Enlarge your vision of how God wants to use you. There is a world waiting for you and waiting for what you have inside you.

God said, I will give you the keys of the kingdom of heaven, whatever you bind on earth will be bound in heaven and whatever you loose on earth will be loosed in heaven.

The one who is in You is greater than the one who is in the world.

You have great authority and power to use for this world ask God for the faith for nations and start praying!

A prayer for the nations

Dear Father,
Thank you that you want me to have a share in your inheritance of the nations. Father, I pray for the nations of this world to come to your light. As your gospel goes forth through the word, media, churches, missionaries and prayer that many will come to a knowledge of you.

I pray that you will open doors for the nations that are closed to the gospel of Jesus Christ and those that walk in darkness will see a great light. I pray especially for the country of ....that your people in that country will be kept safe and protected and increase in number. I pray for a Holy Ghost move of God in that country led by men and women called of God full of faith and the word.

May my prayers and all you have placed within me go out to the four corners of the earth and be a blessing according to your promise over my life.

May the gospel be preached in the whole world before your return.

May the nations of this world become the nations of our God.

May the name of the Lord Jesus be lifted up and proclaimed in every nation of the world.
In Jesus Name,
Amen.

CHAPTER ELEVEN

POWER OF HEAVEN

Prayer for Revival in the Church.

Revive us to trust in You.

Awake, awake O Zion clothe yourself with strength. Shake off your dust; rise up.

Revive us and we will call on your name. Restore us, Lord God Almighty.

Lord, I have heard of your fame; I stand in awe of your deeds, Lord. Repeat them in our day, in our time make them known.

Will you not revive us again that your people may rejoice in you?

I know your deeds, that you are neither cold nor hot. I wish you were either one or the other!

The hour has already come for you to wake up from your slumber.

Wake up sleeper, rise from the dead and Christ will shine on you.

Psalm 80:18 Psalm 85:6
Isaiah 52:1-2 Revelation 3:15
Psalm 80:18 Romans 13:11
Habakkuk 3:2 Ephesians 5:14

Be Ready!

Christ is coming back for a church that is alive, awake and on fire.
We must keep awake in these last days and be like the wise virgins ready when He comes.
Pray that the church will not be found asleep or complacent.
Pray for a Holy Ghost revival that will shake the doorposts of Heaven and earth.

A prayer for revival

Dear Father,
I pray in these last days for your church to awake out of sleep and be filled with fresh passion and power in the Holy Spirit.

I pray there will be a revival in the church of your work, prayer and power.

I pray that Your Holy Spirit will come afresh and stir the church to awake and put on her garments of strength.

I pray the church will rise up a mighty army all over the world with faith in a Great God. Revive us again O God. Restore us and set us on fire with the Holy Spirit. You are building your church and the gates of hell shall not prevail against it.

In Jesus Name,
Amen.

CHAPTER TWELVE

PERSONAL PORTION FROM GOD

Man shall not live on bread alone, but on every (portion) word that comes from the mouth of God.

You are worried about many things. Few things are needed, or indeed only one. Mary has chosen (the best portion) and it will not be taken away from her.

Be still and know that I am God.

Blessed are those who listen to me, watching daily at my gates.

One thing I ask of the Lord, this only do I seek, that I may dwell in the house of the Lord all the days of my life.

If anyone hears my voice and opens the door, I will come in and eat with that person, and they with me.

Seek me and live!

You will fill me with joy in your presence.

I am the good shepherd I know my sheep and my sheep know me. The gatekeeper opens the gate for him, and the sheep listen to his voice. He goes ahead of them and his sheep follow him because they know his voice.

I am the bread of life, whoever comes to me will never go hungry and whoever believes in me in me will never be thirsty. There, above the cover between the two cherubim that are over the ark of the covenant law, I will meet with you.

For where two or three gather in my name, there I am with them.

Matthew 4:4
Luke 10:42
Psalm 46:10
Proverbs 8:34
Psalm 27:4

Revelation 3:20
Psalm 16:11   John 10:
1-10   John 6:3
Matthew 18:20

My Daily Portion

Jesus said there was only one thing really worth being concerned about and that was sitting at His feet listening to Him. Jesus said it was not enough to just feed our bodies every day but we need to feed our spirits by hearing God's word as well.

He said there was a portion in each day for all those who desire to sit with Him. However busy our lives become there will be a time to hear God's voice each day. It is good to pray and share our hearts but it is also important to take a few minutes and listen to what God may want to say to you.

God is always speaking but few take the time to listen to Him in the daily hustle and bustle of life.

God speaks of good rewards for those who seek Him and listen for Him. He says those who listen for Him and watch for Him daily find life and receive favour from the Lord. Everyone can hear from God but it takes practice to listen to the Shepherd's voice. Jesus said His sheep would know His voice and follow Him and not follow another.

If you are not sure how to hear God speaking to you take these next few steps:

1. Find a quiet spot somewhere, a bedroom, garden, church etc.

2. Get your whole being quiet. Stop fidgeting and moving about; get comfortable and focused.

3. Have a pen and paper ready so that you can write down what you believe God is saying to you and He or someone else can confirm the word later.

4. Take authority over any deception the enemy may want to put over your mind.

5. Ask the Holy Spirit to fill your thoughts with His thoughts. Trust God that He wants to communicate and speak to you.

6. You may feel as you begin to sit quiet and listen, that the words are just coming from you and not the Holy Spirit. However, it helps to write it down and ask God to confirm what He has said to you.

7. You may begin to hear only a few words such as 'fear not' or 'I love you' with the Shepherd's voice.

8. Ask God to confirm His word and He will. This could be through the written word, a pastor, or another Christian.

Dear Father,

I am still and waiting for You...........

Made in the USA
Charleston, SC
07 February 2013